The Spectrum Within

Living with Emotions

JD ARDEN

Preface

Emotions are the invisible currents that shape our lives. They guide us, haunt us, uplift us, and sometimes drag us to the depths. Yet, for all their power, emotions are often misunderstood or dismissed—viewed as inconvenient distractions rather than as vital forces. We prefer to speak of logic, of reason, of the mind, because these concepts feel stable, predictable. But the truth is, we are emotional beings first, and it is only by embracing the spectrum of our emotions that we can live fully and authentically.

This book is a guide to navigating that vast emotional terrain. It's not about taming your emotions or keeping them neatly contained. It's about understanding them—learning their language, appreciating their wisdom, and finding ways to coexist with their complexity. Whether it's fear, joy, anger, or sadness, each emotion has something to tell us, something to teach us. The key is to listen.

Our journey begins by diving into each emotion individually, exploring its origins, its purpose, and its impact on our lives. Along the way, we'll uncover how these forces influence our relationships, our choices, and our sense of self. No emotion is without value. Even those that make us uncomfortable have something vital to say. This book is an invitation to embrace it all—the light and the dark, the storm and the calm, the familiar and the unknown. Because it is in this full embrace that we find our truest selves.

Chapter 1: The Emotional Spectrum

Emotions are not neatly labelled boxes to be stored away or put on display when convenient. They are a spectrum—fluid, overlapping, and deeply interwoven with every aspect of our lives. The emotional spectrum stretches from the brightness of joy and love to the shadows of fear and anger, and it's constantly shifting. One moment you're content, and the next, something sparks a deep sense of loss or longing. To understand this spectrum is to understand yourself—because, at your core, you are a creature of emotion.

From the day we are born, emotions shape our experience of the world. The first sensation we feel may be discomfort, a primal scream to announce our arrival. As we grow, those simple cries evolve into a complex emotional tapestry. We learn to smile at warmth, to cry at loss, to feel anger when things aren't fair. We begin to recognize that each emotion serves a purpose, and none are inherently good or bad. They are signals—raw data from our inner selves. They tell us when something needs attention, when boundaries have been crossed, when we are aligned with what we desire, and when we are far from it.

Our culture likes to categorize emotions—good versus bad, positive versus negative. Joy, love, contentment—these are the "good" ones. Anger, sadness, jealousy—they get labeled as "bad." But it's not that simple. Every emotion is part of a larger ecosystem, and each one plays its role. Fear keeps us safe, sadness reminds us of what matters, and even anger can be a force for change. Labeling emotions as good or bad oversimplifies what is inherently complex, ignoring the wisdom that each feeling carries.

Consider fear. Fear is often painted as something to be conquered, something to push through or ignore. But fear is also a protector. It is the emotion that keeps us from dangerous situations, that makes us cautious when the stakes are high. It is deeply wired into our survival. The problem is not fear itself but how we handle it—whether we let it paralyze us or listen to its warning without being consumed. The emotional spectrum is not about erasing fear but about seeing it clearly and responding with understanding.

And then there is joy—the fleeting spark that lights up our days, that makes life feel full. Joy is often elusive, and when it comes, we try to hold onto it tightly. But joy is not meant to be possessed; it's meant to be experienced in its moment and then released. To live with emotional awareness is to understand that joy, like all emotions, is part of a larger ebb and flow. The more we try to force it or cling to it, the more it slips through our fingers. True joy comes from accepting its impermanence, from savoring it while it's there and being grateful even in its absence.

Living with emotions means learning to navigate between extremes— anger that can either destroy or protect, love that can heal or overwhelm, sadness that can weigh us down or deepen our understanding of what we cherish. It means acknowledging that emotions don't fit into neat categories. They exist on a continuum, and more often than not, they overlap, blend, and coexist in ways that defy logic. You can feel immense sadness and a strange sense of peace at the same time. You can be deeply in love yet terrified of what that love might mean. This is the reality of the emotional spectrum—a space where everything can exist all at once.

The first step to living fully with emotions is to understand that they are not the enemy. They are not something to be conquered, minimized, or silenced. They are a part of you, as fundamental as your heartbeat or your breath. They are guides, each with its message. Anger tells you when something is wrong, fear keeps you alert, joy reminds you why life is worth living. To ignore emotions is to ignore yourself. To embrace them is to live in alignment with who you truly are.

In the following chapters, we will take a closer look at each emotion. We'll explore where they come from, what they need, and how we can learn to coexist with them in a way that enriches rather than hinders our lives. Emotions are not always comfortable, but they are always meaningful. The key is not to escape the discomfort but to move through it—to see each emotion as an essential part of the spectrum that makes you human.

Understanding the emotional spectrum is about acceptance—embracing every part of yourself, even the parts that you wish were different. Because in the end, it is this full acceptance that brings us peace, that makes us resilient, and that allows us to live truly authentic lives. The emotional spectrum is vast, unpredictable, and sometimes overwhelming.

But it is also beautiful, and it is yours. Learn to navigate it, and you learn to navigate yourself.

Chapter 2: The Language of Emotion

Emotions are the silent language of our inner world. They do not speak in words or logical phrases, yet they communicate with profound clarity. They speak through bodily sensations—tightness in the chest, warmth in the belly, the rush of adrenaline. They speak through instinctual reactions, through tears, laughter, clenched jaws, and a thousand other subtle signals that convey what words cannot. Understanding the language of emotions means learning to listen to the body and interpret the signals it sends. It's a language that requires us to go beyond the rational, to engage with what is deeply felt but not always understood.

The body and mind are not separate entities. Emotions exist in this intersection, straddling the physical and the psychological. When you feel anxious, you may notice your heart rate increase or your palms begin to sweat. Anger might manifest as a flush of heat in your face or a knot in your stomach. These physical sensations are the body's way of expressing the emotional energy that is moving through you. Ignoring these signals doesn't make them disappear; it simply pushes them underground where they often manifest in other, more harmful ways— through chronic stress, fatigue, or even illness.

Learning to read the language of emotion is about recognizing these bodily cues for what they are: messages. Your body is constantly communicating with you, giving you information about your environment, your relationships, and your inner needs. When you're in a situation that doesn't feel right, your body knows before your conscious mind does. You might feel tense, uneasy, or instinctively want to leave. That feeling is your emotional radar, and paying attention to it is the first step towards understanding and respecting your own boundaries.

Emotions also speak through patterns. If you find yourself feeling the same emotion repeatedly in similar situations, it's likely that there's a message there that needs attention. For instance, if you consistently feel resentment when dealing with a particular person, it may be a sign that your boundaries are being crossed. If sadness arises each time you revisit a certain memory, it's telling you there is something there that hasn't been fully processed. Recognizing these patterns is a crucial part of emotional awareness, as it allows you to address the root causes rather than simply managing symptoms.

The language of emotion is not always comfortable. There are feelings we instinctively resist—anger, jealousy, fear—because we have learned to label them as negative or harmful. We're taught to suppress them, to maintain composure, to stay "positive." But emotions do not vanish just because we ignore them. Instead, they fester, transform, and sometimes come back stronger. Emotional suppression is a way of denying ourselves a part of our experience, and in the long run, it often leads to greater pain. Anger, when ignored, can turn into bitterness. Sadness, left unexpressed, can become depression. Understanding emotional language means giving each feeling the space to be acknowledged without judgment.

Emotional language also involves context. A smile can mean many things—joy, politeness, even discomfort. A tear can represent sadness, but also relief, laughter, or frustration. Emotions are not simple; they are complex and layered. Part of understanding emotional language is learning to decode these nuances. It means asking deeper questions: Why am I feeling this way now? What triggered this emotion? Is this feeling a reaction to something present, or does it have its roots in past experiences? Often, emotions are not just about what's happening in the moment but are tied to patterns and memories that go far deeper.

Another key aspect of emotional language is the understanding of mixed emotions. Rarely do we feel one emotion in isolation. More often than not, emotions blend together—fear mixed with excitement, love tinged with jealousy, joy shadowed by anxiety. The human experience is one of emotional complexity, and learning to sit with this complexity without needing to simplify it is essential. We are taught to categorize emotions neatly, but life is messy, and emotions reflect that messiness. Understanding mixed emotions means accepting that conflicting feelings can coexist and that this coexistence is a natural part of being human.

To learn the language of emotion is to cultivate emotional intelligence. Emotional intelligence is not just about recognizing emotions in ourselves but also about being attuned to the emotions of others. It's about empathy—understanding that just as our feelings are valid, so are those of the people around us. Emotions are what connect us to others.

They are the basis of compassion, understanding, and genuine connection. By learning to understand our own emotions, we become better equipped to navigate relationships, to communicate honestly, and to respond to others in a way that is caring and authentic.

Ultimately, the language of emotion is about trust. Trusting that your feelings have value. Trusting that your body knows what it needs. Trusting that emotions, even the difficult ones, are there for a reason. It's about listening—not just with your mind but with your whole being. Emotions are guides. They may not always be convenient, and they may sometimes point us in directions we'd rather not go, but they are always speaking truth. The question is, are you willing to listen?

Chapter 3: Fear: The Shadow We Carry

Fear is an emotion that most people would rather avoid. It's uncomfortable, unsettling, and often paralyzing. But fear is also one of the most fundamental parts of being human. It has kept us alive for millennia, protecting us from danger and pushing us to make decisions that ensure our survival. Fear is a natural response to the unknown, to the possibility of loss or harm. And while it is easy to view fear as an enemy, it's actually one of our most loyal protectors—if we learn how to listen to it.

The problem with fear isn't that it exists. The problem is how we react to it. Our instincts tell us to either run from it or to fight it tooth and nail. In many ways, fear brings out our most primal instincts—the fight-or-flight response. This response served our ancestors well when they faced the very real dangers of predators or hostile environments. Today, however, most of the fears we face are not life-threatening, yet our bodies and minds react as if they are. The challenge is not to get rid of fear but to learn how to coexist with it without letting it control our lives.

Fear is often rooted in uncertainty. We fear what we don't know, what we can't predict, and what we can't control. It's why fear often rears its head in times of change—new jobs, new relationships, new responsibilities. It's not necessarily the change itself that terrifies us, but the uncertainty that comes with it. The "what ifs" that spin out of control in our minds. What if I fail? What if I make a mistake? What if I'm not good enough? These fears feed on uncertainty, growing larger the more we try to ignore them. The key to dealing with this type of fear is not to eliminate uncertainty—that's impossible—but to learn to sit with it, to accept that we can't know everything and that that's okay.

There's also the fear of pain—emotional, physical, and psychological. We fear being hurt, and so we build walls. We avoid vulnerability, we keep our distance, we tell ourselves that it's safer not to care too much or not to try too hard. But this avoidance has a cost. When we let the fear of pain dictate our choices, we also cut ourselves off from the possibility of joy, connection, and growth. To live fully is to accept that pain is part of the deal. Fear tells us to stay small, to stay safe, but true fulfillment comes from pushing past that fear, from being willing to face discomfort for the sake of something greater.

Another insidious form of fear is the fear of failure. This fear can be paralyzing, holding us back from pursuing our dreams, from taking risks, and from stepping out of our comfort zones. The fear of failure is often tied to a deeper fear—the fear of not being enough. We fear that if we fail, it will confirm our worst suspicions about ourselves, that we are not capable or worthy. This fear is powerful because it strikes at the core of our self-esteem. The only way to combat it is to change our relationship with failure. Failure is not a reflection of our worth. It is simply a part of the learning process, an inevitable step on the road to success. When we learn to see failure as feedback rather than as a verdict on our value, fear loses much of its power.

Fear also thrives on isolation. When we face our fears alone, they seem insurmountable. But when we share our fears, when we speak them aloud, they lose some of their grip. There is immense power in vulnerability, in admitting that we are scared and allowing others to support us. Fear makes us feel like we are the only ones struggling, but the truth is, everyone feels fear. It is one of the most universal human experiences. By opening up about our fears, we not only lighten our own burden but also create space for others to do the same.

One of the most effective ways to deal with fear is through exposure. Avoidance only reinforces fear, making it grow stronger in the dark corners of our mind. But when we face what we fear, even in small doses, we begin to dismantle its power. This doesn't mean diving headfirst into your deepest fears without preparation. It means taking gradual steps— exposing yourself to what scares you in manageable ways, proving to yourself that you can handle it. Each small victory over fear builds confidence, and slowly, fear's hold begins to loosen.

At its core, fear is not something to be eliminated; it is something to be understood. It is a shadow that follows us, but it also serves a purpose. It shows us where we feel vulnerable, where we need to grow, where we are stepping into something new and challenging. Fear is a sign that we are alive, that we are stepping outside the familiar. The goal is not to banish fear but to keep moving forward despite it, to let it be a part of our journey without letting it dictate the route.

Fear is a teacher, if we are willing to learn from it. It teaches us about our limits, but more importantly, it teaches us how to expand those limits. It shows us what matters to us—because we don't fear losing things that are unimportant. Fear marks the edges of our comfort zone, and beyond those edges lies growth. To understand fear is to understand the boundaries you have set for yourself, and to know that you have the power to push beyond them, one step at a time.

Chapter 4: Joy: The Light That Lifts

Joy is the light that breaks through the shadows. It is fleeting, elusive, and often arrives unannounced, but its impact is undeniable. Unlike fear or anger, which command our attention with their intensity, joy can be subtle—gentle as a breeze, warm as the sun on a spring morning. It's the feeling that makes life feel worthwhile, even if just for a moment. Joy is often treated as something that happens to us, but in reality, it's something we can nurture, something we can learn to cultivate by being fully present and open to the small miracles of everyday life.

Joy doesn't demand grand events or monumental achievements. It lives in the quiet moments—in the sound of laughter, in the warmth of a hug, in the beauty of a sunset. To experience joy, we have to be open to it. This might sound simple, but it requires an intentional shift. So much of our time is spent worrying, planning, analyzing—keeping us detached from the present moment. Joy, however, only exists in the present. It's found in the now, not in the worries about tomorrow or the regrets of yesterday. This means that to feel joy, we have to let go of our endless preoccupations and allow ourselves to be where we are, as we are.

A barrier to joy is the belief that it must be earned—that we have to work hard enough, achieve enough, or be deserving enough before we can experience it. But joy is not a reward for good behavior. It's a birthright, a fundamental part of being human. Children understand this instinctively—they laugh, play, and find wonder in the smallest things without worrying whether they have "earned" it. As we grow older, we often lose touch with this innate sense of joy, replacing it with an idea that we must meet certain criteria before we can be happy. The truth is, joy doesn't have prerequisites. It's available to all of us, right here, right now, if we are willing to accept it.

Joy is also deeply tied to connection. When we share experiences with others, when we feel understood or see someone we care about light up with happiness, joy is magnified. It's contagious, spreading from person to person, reminding us that we are not alone. This is why moments of collective joy—celebrations, laughter among friends, acts of kindness—are so powerful. They bind us together, creating a sense of unity and shared humanity. In a world that often feels divided, joy reminds us of our common ground, of our capacity for compassion and connection.

But joy is not without its challenges. For many of us, there is a fear attached to joy—the fear that it won't last, that the moment we let ourselves feel happy, something will come along to take it away. This fear can prevent us from fully embracing joy, keeping us always on guard, waiting for the other shoe to drop. This is sometimes called "foreboding joy," the feeling that happiness is too good to be true. But this fear doesn't protect us from pain—it only robs us of the full experience of joy when it's present. To embrace joy is to accept its impermanence, to allow ourselves to feel happiness without clinging to it or fearing its end.

Cultivating joy is about being intentional—about recognizing the moments that bring light into your life and allowing yourself to savor them. It's about gratitude, about noticing the good that exists even in difficult times. Joy doesn't mean ignoring pain or pretending that everything is perfect. It means finding the light that coexists with the darkness, no matter how small, and letting it lift you, even if just for a moment. It's a practice, one that requires us to be open, vulnerable, and present. But the reward is immense—a life that feels fuller, richer, and more connected.

Chapter 5: Anger: The Fire Within

Anger is a powerful emotion, often misunderstood and frequently feared. It's a fire—intense, consuming, and sometimes destructive. But anger is not inherently bad. It's not something to be ashamed of or something that needs to be eradicated. Anger is an essential part of being human. It tells us when something is wrong, when our boundaries have been crossed, when there is an injustice that needs addressing. The challenge is not in feeling anger but in how we respond to it. Learning to harness the energy of anger without letting it take control is one of the most important skills we can develop.

At its core, anger is a response to perceived threat or injustice. It's the emotion that arises when we feel wronged, when our values are violated, or when we see someone we care about being mistreated. In many ways, anger is a protector. It is what motivates us to stand up for ourselves, to fight for what we believe in, to draw lines that shouldn't be crossed. But when left unchecked, anger can also be destructive—it can cause harm, damage relationships, and lead us to make decisions we later regret. This is why understanding anger is crucial. It's not about suppressing it, but about channeling it in a way that is constructive rather than destructive.

One of the biggest misconceptions about anger is that it is inherently negative. Many of us were taught from a young age that anger is something to be avoided—that expressing anger makes us "bad" or "unpleasant." As a result, many people suppress their anger, pushing it down until it either festers or explodes. Suppressed anger doesn't go away; it often finds other ways to manifest, whether through passive-aggressiveness, bitterness, or even physical symptoms like headaches or tension. True emotional health requires acknowledging anger when it arises and finding healthy ways to express it.

Anger, when understood and managed well, can be a force for positive change. Think of the many movements for social justice that have been fueled by anger—anger at inequality, at discrimination, at the mistreatment of others. This kind of anger is righteous; it's the fire that propels people to take action, to demand better, to fight for a fairer world. When anger is directed towards addressing an injustice rather than harming others, it becomes a catalyst for progress. The key is to channel that energy constructively, to ensure that it doesn't lead to blind rage but to thoughtful, purposeful action.

To understand your own anger, you must first learn to recognize its signs. Anger often begins in the body—a tightening of the chest, a clenching of the jaw, a surge of adrenaline. These physical sensations are the first clues that anger is present, and recognizing them is the first step to managing it. Once you notice anger arising, take a moment to pause. Breathe deeply. Give yourself space to feel the anger without reacting impulsively. This doesn't mean ignoring it—it means acknowledging its presence while giving yourself the time to decide how to respond.

A powerful way to manage anger is to examine what lies beneath it. Anger is often a surface emotion, masking deeper feelings like fear, hurt, or frustration. If you find yourself angry, ask yourself: What am I really feeling? Am I scared? Am I hurt? Am I feeling disrespected? By getting to the root of your anger, you can respond more effectively. Rather than lashing out, you can address the real issue—whether that means setting a boundary, communicating your feelings, or taking action to change a situation.

Healthy expression of anger involves communicating clearly and respectfully. It means using "I" statements—"I feel angry because..." rather than "You made me angry." This shifts the focus from blame to understanding, creating space for dialogue rather than confrontation. It's about expressing what you need without attacking the other person. Anger that is expressed in this way can actually strengthen relationships, as it allows both parties to understand each other better and to address underlying issues rather than letting resentment build.

There is also value in physical release when dealing with anger. Anger is energy, and sometimes that energy needs a physical outlet. Exercise, punching a pillow, yelling in a safe space—these are all ways to release pent-up anger without causing harm. The goal is not to deny the intensity of what you're feeling but to find ways to let it out that are safe and constructive.

Anger is a fire, and like any fire, it can either destroy or warm, depending on how it is used. The key is to respect its power. To understand that it is neither inherently good nor bad but simply a part of who we are. Anger tells us that something matters, that something needs to change. By listening to that message and choosing how we respond, we can turn anger from a destructive force into a powerful tool for growth, change, and deeper self-understanding.

Chapter 6: Sadness: The Weight of Loss

Sadness is often seen as the emotion to avoid at all costs. It's heavy, lingering, and, unlike joy or even anger, doesn't always spur us into action. It slows us down, makes us introspective, and reminds us of everything we've lost or never had. But sadness is more than just a negative emotion—it is an essential aspect of the human experience, and one that, if approached correctly, can lead to a deeper understanding of ourselves, of what we cherish, and of how we heal.

Sadness is a response to loss. That loss could be tangible—a loved one, a relationship, a job. Or it could be something less concrete—lost opportunities, lost dreams, or even the slow erosion of time. Unlike fear or anger, which tend to ignite a sense of urgency, sadness often brings with it a sense of stillness. It forces us to stop, to sit with our feelings, to grieve. This stillness is necessary; it's how we process what we've lost. It's how we honor the importance of what or who was lost, allowing us to integrate the experience into our lives rather than pretending it never happened.

The discomfort of sadness comes from our resistance to it. Society teaches us to smile through our pain, to focus on the positive, to avoid being "too emotional." But in doing so, we deny ourselves the chance to heal. Sadness needs to be felt. It demands acknowledgment. The tears, the heaviness in the chest, the desire to withdraw—these are all part of the process. They are the body's way of releasing emotional pain, of allowing us to move forward rather than staying stuck. When we suppress sadness, we deny ourselves that release, which can lead to a buildup of unresolved grief that affects every part of our lives.

Sadness also plays a crucial role in empathy and connection. When we allow ourselves to feel sadness, we open ourselves up to the pain of others. We become more compassionate, more understanding, more willing to sit with someone else's discomfort without rushing to "fix" it. Empathy is born from shared experience. It's in our own moments of sadness that we learn to truly understand what others are going through.

This kind of empathy creates deep, meaningful connections, reminding us that, even in our darkest times, we are not alone.

Grief is a specific form of sadness that often feels overwhelming, all-consuming. It's the kind of sadness that doesn't have a timeline. It comes in waves—sometimes predictable, sometimes not. Grief is a testament to love. The depth of our grief reflects the depth of our connection, the value of what was lost. It's not something that can be rushed or minimized. Grief demands time, patience, and, most importantly, acceptance. It's not about "getting over" a loss but about learning to live alongside it, allowing the sadness to coexist with other emotions—joy, love, even hope.

Sadness is also a great teacher. It teaches us about impermanence, about the fleeting nature of life. It reminds us of what truly matters, of who and what we care about. In moments of sadness, we often find clarity—realizing what we need, what we've taken for granted, what we want to change. Sadness strips away the superficial, leaving us with the raw, unfiltered truth of our lives. It's in these moments that we learn the most about ourselves, about our resilience, and about our capacity for love and healing.

The key to navigating sadness is to allow yourself to feel it without becoming consumed by it. It's a delicate balance—acknowledging the heaviness while also recognizing that it won't last forever. Sadness is a part of the emotional spectrum, but it's not the entirety of it. Even in the depths of sadness, moments of light can still break through—a kind word from a friend, a beautiful sunset, a memory that brings a smile. These moments don't erase the sadness, but they remind us that life is complex and that joy and sorrow often coexist.

Ultimately, sadness is not something to be feared or avoided. It is a natural, inevitable part of life. By embracing it, by allowing ourselves to grieve, to mourn, to feel deeply, we open ourselves up to the possibility of healing. We honor what we have lost and, in doing so, create space for new growth, for new connections, for new beginnings. Sadness is heavy, yes, but it is also profoundly human. To feel sadness is to be alive, to care deeply, and to understand the value of what we have, even when it's gone.

Chapter 7: Love: The Binding Force

Love is perhaps the most celebrated of all human emotions. It is the force that binds us, that drives us to connect, to sacrifice, to grow. Love is often idealized—portrayed in books, movies, and songs as an all-powerful, flawless emotion that conquers all. But in reality, love is far more complex. It is both beautiful and challenging, uplifting and terrifying, comforting and unsettling. To truly understand love, we must be willing to see it for what it is: a deeply human, often imperfect emotion that requires vulnerability, effort, and courage.

Love takes many forms—romantic love, familial love, love for friends, love for oneself. Each type of love is unique, yet they all share common elements: connection, empathy, care, and a desire to see another being flourish. Romantic love, for example, is often filled with passion, excitement, and a deep sense of connection. It's the kind of love that can make us feel invincible one moment and utterly vulnerable the next. It's a love that demands intimacy, trust, and the willingness to let someone see us as we truly are—flaws and all.

Familial love is different. It's rooted in history, in shared experiences, in a bond that often exists from birth. This kind of love is not always easy—it can be filled with expectations, misunderstandings, and old wounds. But it is also enduring, resilient, and often unconditional. It's the kind of love that persists even in the face of conflict, the kind that shows up when it matters most. Familial love is about acceptance—seeing each other not as perfect but as imperfect beings worthy of love regardless.

Love for friends is a love of choice. Unlike family, we choose our friends, and they choose us. This kind of love is built on mutual respect, shared interests, and the joy of companionship. Friendships are often the relationships that sustain us through the ups and downs of life. They provide support, laughter, and a sense of belonging. Friendship is a form of love that is often overlooked or undervalued, but it is just as powerful and necessary as any other. It's the love that reminds us we don't have to face life alone.

And then there is self-love—the most challenging and perhaps the most important form of love. Self-love is about accepting yourself as you are, with all your flaws, mistakes, and imperfections. It's about treating yourself with the same kindness and compassion that you offer to others. For many, self-love is difficult because it requires confronting the parts of yourself that you'd rather ignore. It means forgiving yourself for past mistakes, setting boundaries, and recognizing your own worth. Self-love is not selfish; it is the foundation upon which all other love is built. Without it, we struggle to fully give or receive love from others.

Love is not always easy. It requires effort, compromise, and, at times, sacrifice. It's about showing up, even when it's hard, even when you're tired, even when the person you love has hurt you. It's about choosing to care, to forgive, to nurture. Love is not a passive feeling; it is an active choice—a decision to invest in someone, to prioritize their well-being, to share your life with them. It is this choice that makes love so powerful. It is not something that just happens to us; it is something we create, nurture, and grow.

But love is also scary. To love is to open yourself up to the possibility of loss. It is to make yourself vulnerable, to risk rejection, to face the uncertainty of the future. The deeper we love, the greater the risk—and yet, we do it anyway. Because love, despite its risks, is what gives life meaning. It is what makes the struggles worthwhile, what gives us hope, what makes us feel alive. Love is the binding force that connects us to others, that reminds us we are not alone, that we are seen, valued, and cherished.

Love is not perfect, and it doesn't have to be. It is messy, unpredictable, and, at times, challenging. It can bring immense joy, but it can also bring pain. To love is to accept both—the light and the dark, the joy and the heartbreak. It is to recognize that love is not about finding someone who is perfect, but about seeing the imperfections and loving anyway. It is about growth—both personal and shared. Love challenges us to be better, to let go of our ego, to put someone else's needs before our own, to grow together.

Ultimately, love is what binds us to each other and to ourselves. It is the force that connects us to something greater than ourselves, that gives us purpose, that fills our lives with meaning. It is not always easy, and it is rarely simple, but it is always worth it. To love is to be human. It is to embrace the messiness of life, to open yourself up to joy, pain, connection, and growth. Love is the thread that weaves through the emotional spectrum, tying it all together, reminding us that, at the end of the day, what matters most is not what we have, but who we have beside us, and the love we choose to share.

Chapter 8: Guilt and Shame: The Hidden Burdens

Guilt and shame are two of the heaviest emotions we carry, often lurking in the background, shaping our thoughts, our behaviors, and our sense of self-worth. They are burdens that can weigh us down, keeping us trapped in the past, unable to move forward. Though closely related, guilt and shame are distinct: guilt is the feeling that we have done something wrong, while shame is the belief that we are fundamentally flawed because of it. Guilt says, "I made a mistake." Shame says, "I am a mistake." Understanding these differences and learning to navigate these emotions is crucial for emotional well-being and growth.

Guilt can serve a useful purpose—it's a signal that we've violated our own moral code, that our actions are out of alignment with our values. It pushes us to make amends, to learn from our mistakes, to grow into better versions of ourselves. Guilt, when handled properly, can be a positive force for change. It encourages accountability and helps us maintain our relationships by acknowledging when we've hurt someone and taking steps to repair the damage.

However, guilt can also be misplaced. Sometimes we feel guilty for things that were beyond our control, for other people's choices, or for simply being who we are. This type of guilt is not constructive; it's a weight we carry unnecessarily, often because we've been conditioned to believe that we are responsible for the feelings or actions of others. Learning to differentiate between valid guilt and misplaced guilt is essential. Valid guilt should be acted upon—with apologies, changes in behavior, or making amends. Misplaced guilt, on the other hand, needs to be let go, as it serves no purpose other than to drain our energy and keep us stuck.

Shame, unlike guilt, often has no clear path to resolution. It's deeply tied to our sense of identity, making us feel fundamentally unworthy or unlovable. Shame is often instilled in us from a young age, whether through critical parents, bullying, societal expectations, or traumatic experiences. It's the voice that tells us we are not enough—that we are broken, defective, beyond redemption. This is why shame is so toxic: it attacks the core of who we are, making it incredibly difficult to find self-acceptance or to believe we deserve love and compassion.

The first step to dealing with shame is to bring it into the light. Shame thrives in secrecy. The more we hide it, the stronger it becomes. By talking about our shame, by sharing our stories with people we trust, we begin to dismantle its power. Vulnerability is the antidote to shame. When we open up, when we allow ourselves to be seen in our entirety—flaws, mistakes, and all—we start to see that we are not alone. We see that others have felt the same, that we are not uniquely flawed, but simply human. This shared understanding helps to break the isolation that shame creates and allows us to begin the process of healing.

Self-compassion is also a powerful tool for dealing with guilt and shame. It's about treating yourself with the same kindness and understanding that you would offer a friend. Instead of beating yourself up for your mistakes, recognize that everyone makes mistakes—that imperfection is a part of being human. When you approach yourself with compassion, you create a space where guilt can be processed constructively, where shame can be softened, and where you can begin to accept yourself as you are, without the weight of constant self-criticism.

Ultimately, guilt and shame are emotions that ask us to look inward, to confront parts of ourselves that we might rather ignore. But they do not have to define us. By understanding their origins, by differentiating between what is helpful and what is harmful, and by approaching ourselves with compassion, we can transform these hidden burdens into opportunities for growth and connection. We can learn to let go of what we cannot change, to forgive ourselves, and to move forward with a sense of hope and worthiness.

Chapter 9: Curiosity: The Desire to Know

Curiosity is one of the most fundamental human emotions—it's the driving force behind learning, discovery, and innovation. It's the spark that pushes us to explore the unknown, to ask questions, to seek understanding. Curiosity is often seen as a positive emotion, and for good reason: it keeps us engaged with the world, encourages growth, and leads us to new experiences. But like all emotions, curiosity has its complexities. It can be both liberating and unsettling, both a source of joy and a path to uncomfortable truths.

At its core, curiosity is about the desire to know. It's what compels children to ask "why" a hundred times a day, what drives scientists to explore the mysteries of the universe, what pushes artists to experiment with new forms of expression. Curiosity is the antidote to stagnation. It keeps our minds open, our perspectives broad, and our lives rich with possibility. When we are curious, we are willing to step outside our comfort zones, to risk being wrong, to admit that we don't have all the answers. It's this openness to uncertainty that makes curiosity such a powerful force for growth.

Curiosity is also deeply tied to empathy. When we are curious about other people, we are more likely to listen to their stories, to understand their experiences, to see the world through their eyes. Empathy begins with curiosity—the willingness to ask questions, to learn about someone else's perspective, to care about their feelings and experiences. In relationships, curiosity keeps us connected. It keeps us from making assumptions, from taking each other for granted. When we remain curious about our loved ones, we continue to learn about them, to grow with them, and to deepen our connection.

However, curiosity can also lead us into uncomfortable territory. It can push us to confront truths we might rather ignore—about ourselves, about others, about the world. Sometimes, the answers we find are not what we hoped for. Curiosity can reveal flaws, uncover lies, or lead us to question beliefs that once felt secure. This is the double-edged nature of curiosity: it can bring wonder and delight, but it can also bring discomfort and doubt. Yet, even when curiosity leads us to difficult places, it is still valuable. It is better to know, to understand, to face the truth, than to live in ignorance or denial.

Curiosity is also what keeps us adaptable. The world is constantly changing, and those who are curious are better equipped to navigate these changes. They are the ones who ask questions, who learn new skills, who are not afraid to try something different. Curiosity keeps us from becoming rigid, from clinging to outdated ideas or practices. It encourages innovation, creativity, and progress. Whether it's in our personal lives or in society at large, curiosity is what drives evolution—it's what moves us forward, even when the path is uncertain.

To cultivate curiosity, we must first let go of the fear of not knowing. So often, we are afraid to ask questions because we don't want to appear ignorant, or because we fear what the answers might reveal. But true curiosity requires a willingness to be vulnerable, to admit that we don't have all the answers, and to be open to whatever we might discover. It's about embracing the unknown, not as something to be feared, but as something to be explored.

Curiosity also requires us to be present. When our minds are preoccupied with worries about the future or regrets about the past, it's difficult to be curious. Curiosity thrives in the here and now—in noticing what's around us, in paying attention to what's happening, in being engaged with the present moment. By cultivating mindfulness, by slowing down and really observing, we create the space for curiosity to flourish.

Ultimately, curiosity is what makes life interesting. It's what turns the mundane into the extraordinary, what transforms routine into adventure. It's the desire to learn, to grow, to experience, to understand. Curiosity keeps us young at heart, no matter our age. It keeps us connected—to ourselves, to others, to the world. It's the emotion that asks us to keep exploring, to keep asking "why," to keep seeking the beauty and mystery that life has to offer.

In a world that often values certainty and control, curiosity is a reminder that it's okay not to have all the answers. It's okay to wonder, to explore, to be wrong, to change your mind. Curiosity invites us to live with an open heart and an open mind, to embrace the unknown not as something to fear but as something to be discovered. It's the desire to know, to understand, to connect—and it is, without a doubt, one of the greatest gifts of being human.

Chapter 10: Jealousy and Envy: The Green-Eyed Emotions

Jealousy and envy are emotions that most of us have felt, yet we rarely like to admit to. They are often labeled as "ugly" or "negative," feelings we should avoid or suppress. But jealousy and envy are as much a part of the human experience as love, joy, or sadness. They arise from deeply rooted desires—desires for belonging, for recognition, for security. To understand these emotions is to understand a fundamental aspect of what it means to be human: our yearning for connection and worth.

Jealousy typically involves a perceived threat to something we already have—our relationships, our status, our place in someone's life. It comes from a fear of losing what is valuable to us. Envy, on the other hand, arises when we see something in someone else's life that we wish we had. It is the feeling of lack, the belief that someone else has what we desire, and that their gain is somehow a reflection of our inadequacy. Both emotions are rooted in comparison, in measuring our worth against others, and in the fear that we are not enough as we are.

The discomfort of jealousy and envy often leads to attempts to ignore or hide these feelings. We convince ourselves that we shouldn't feel this way, that it's wrong or embarrassing. But like all emotions, jealousy and envy serve a purpose. They are indicators that something important to us feels threatened or unfulfilled. Instead of dismissing them, we need to look deeper and understand what they are telling us. Are we feeling insecure in a relationship? Do we fear losing someone's love or attention? Are we unhappy with where we are in life compared to others? These emotions can be valuable guides, pointing us towards the areas where we need to grow, heal, or make changes.

Jealousy is often tied to a fear of inadequacy. When we feel jealous, we are afraid that we are not enough—that someone else will be better, more attractive, more successful, more deserving of what we value. This fear can lead to possessiveness, mistrust, and attempts to control the people or things we care about. But jealousy can also be an opportunity to address these insecurities. Instead of focusing outward—on the person or situation that triggers the jealousy—we can look inward. What is it about ourselves that feels inadequate? How can we work on building our own sense of self-worth, independent of external validation?

Envy, similarly, arises from comparison. We see someone else's success, happiness, or achievements, and we feel a sense of lack. Envy tells us about our own unfulfilled desires—about the things we want but do not yet have. This can be painful, especially when we feel that what we want is out of reach. But envy can also be a motivator. It can push us to take action, to strive for the things we desire, to improve ourselves. The key is to let envy inspire us rather than consume us. Instead of resenting someone for what they have, we can use that feeling to understand what we truly want and to set goals to achieve it.

Both jealousy and envy become toxic when they lead to resentment, bitterness, or attempts to undermine others. They can damage relationships, fuel hatred, and create a cycle of negativity that keeps us stuck. The way out is through self-awareness and compassion. We need to recognize that these feelings are normal, that they do not make us "bad" people, and that we have the power to respond to them in a healthy way. By acknowledging jealousy and envy without judgment, we can begin to transform them. We can focus on what they reveal about our needs and desires, and take steps to address those underlying issues.

In relationships, jealousy often stems from insecurity and fear of loss. To address jealousy, communication is key. Instead of letting jealousy fester, it's important to talk about these feelings with your partner or loved one. Expressing vulnerability—admitting that you feel insecure or afraid—can be difficult, but it is also incredibly powerful. It opens the door to understanding, to reassurance, to working together to strengthen the relationship. Jealousy is not inherently destructive; it is how we handle it that determines whether it will harm or help us.

In the same vein, overcoming envy requires a shift in perspective. Instead of viewing someone else's success as a reflection of our own lack, we can choose to see it as proof of what is possible. Someone else's happiness or achievements do not diminish our own potential. By celebrating others, by being genuinely happy for their success, we can cultivate a mindset of abundance rather than scarcity. This doesn't mean denying our own desires—it means recognizing that there is enough success, love, and happiness to go around, and that someone else's gain does not equate to our loss.

Jealousy and envy are often portrayed as negative, shameful emotions. But in truth, they are deeply human. They reflect our desires, our fears, our yearning for connection and recognition. By understanding these emotions, by facing them with honesty and compassion, we can learn from them. We can use them as catalysts for growth, for strengthening our relationships, for pursuing our goals. Instead of letting jealousy and envy control us, we can transform them—turning them into opportunities for deeper self-awareness, greater connection, and positive change.

Chapter 11: Calm: Finding Peace Amidst the Storm

In a world that seems to be constantly in motion—filled with demands, stressors, and uncertainties—calm can feel like an elusive state, something we can only hope to experience in rare, fleeting moments. Yet, calm is not something that happens by chance; it is something that can be cultivated. It is a state of mind, a way of approaching the chaos of life with steadiness, clarity, and resilience. Finding calm is about creating an inner sanctuary, a place within ourselves that remains untouched even when everything around us feels like it is falling apart.

Calm begins with the breath. It sounds simple, almost too simple, but the breath is one of the most powerful tools we have to regulate our emotional state. When we are stressed or anxious, our breath becomes shallow, our heart rate increases, and our body goes into fight-or-flight mode. By consciously slowing down our breathing, by taking deep, measured breaths, we send a signal to our nervous system that we are safe. This activates the parasympathetic nervous system—the "rest and digest" response—which helps to bring our body and mind back into balance. It is a simple, yet profoundly effective way to bring ourselves back to a state of calm.

Calm is also about perspective. Often, what creates stress and anxiety is not the situation itself but the way we perceive it. We get caught up in worst-case scenarios, in what-ifs, in the belief that everything is urgent and that we must have all the answers right now. Calm requires us to step back, to take a broader view, to recognize that not everything is as critical as it seems in the heat of the moment. It's about learning to differentiate between what is within our control and what is not, and letting go of the need to control everything. Calm is not about denying the difficulties of life—it's about facing them with a clear head and an open heart.

Another important aspect of calm is acceptance. So much of our inner turmoil comes from resistance—resisting what is, wishing things were different, fighting against reality. Acceptance does not mean giving up or resigning ourselves to a situation; it means acknowledging what is happening without judgment, without adding layers of emotional reactivity. It means recognizing that there are things we cannot change, and that peace comes from accepting that reality rather than exhausting ourselves in an unwinnable battle. Acceptance creates space for calm because it allows us to stop struggling against the inevitable and instead focus on what we can do, here and now.

Calm is also about boundaries. In a world that often glorifies busyness, it's easy to fall into the trap of overcommitment—saying yes to everything, taking on more than we can handle, constantly being available. This kind of lifestyle leaves little room for calm. To find peace, we need to create boundaries—boundaries with our time, our energy, our relationships. This means learning to say no, to prioritize what truly matters, to carve out space for rest and reflection. Boundaries are not selfish; they are essential for our well-being. By setting boundaries, we protect our inner calm, allowing us to show up fully for the things and people that matter most.

Practicing mindfulness is another powerful way to cultivate calm. Mindfulness is about being present—fully present—in whatever we are doing, without judgment. It's about bringing our attention to the here and now, rather than getting lost in worries about the future or regrets about the past. When we are mindful, we are able to approach each moment with clarity, with openness, with a sense of curiosity rather than judgment. This presence of mind naturally creates a sense of calm because it brings us into direct contact with what is real, rather than what is imagined or feared.

Finding calm also involves letting go—letting go of perfectionism, of the need to be in control, of unrealistic expectations. Perfectionism is the enemy of calm; it keeps us in a state of constant striving, always focusing on what is wrong, what needs fixing, what isn't good enough. To find calm, we must be willing to let go of the idea that we need to be perfect, that everything needs to go according to plan, that we must always be in control. True calm comes from embracing imperfection, from recognizing that life is messy, that we are imperfect, and that that is okay.

Calm is not a destination; it is a practice. It is something we return to, again and again, even when we get pulled away by the storms of life. It is about creating habits—daily practices that help us cultivate a sense of peace. This might include meditation, time in nature, journaling, deep breathing, or simply taking a moment each day to pause and be still. These practices help to anchor us, to bring us back to ourselves, to remind us that, no matter what is happening around us, we have the power to create a sense of calm within.

In a world filled with noise, calm is a radical act. It is a refusal to be swept away by the chaos, a decision to create peace within ourselves. It is not about avoiding the storms of life but about finding a way to stand steady in the midst of them. Calm is the choice to breathe, to let go, to be present, to accept what is, and to focus on what truly matters. It is the reminder that, even amidst the storm, we have the power to create a place of stillness within.

Chapter 12: Emotional Complexity: When Feelings Collide

Emotions are rarely simple. More often than not, we experience a blend of feelings—sometimes even contradictory ones—all at once. This emotional complexity is part of what makes us human, and yet, it can also be confusing and overwhelming. How do we make sense of feeling happy and sad at the same time, or feeling both excitement and fear in equal measure? Understanding emotional complexity is about learning to hold multiple emotions without judgment, to accept that our feelings do not have to make perfect sense, and that it's possible to experience seemingly opposite emotions simultaneously.

Life is complex, and so are our emotional responses to it. Take, for example, the experience of starting a new job. You might feel proud of yourself for achieving something you worked hard for, excited about the opportunities ahead, anxious about the unknown, and even a bit sad to be leaving behind the familiar. All these emotions coexist, and none of them are wrong. They all reflect different aspects of the experience, and together, they create a richer, more nuanced understanding of what that moment means to you.

Emotional complexity also plays a role in relationships. You can love someone deeply and still feel frustrated with them. You can feel grateful for their presence in your life while also feeling hurt by something they said. These conflicting emotions do not cancel each other out; rather, they reflect the depth and multifaceted nature of human relationships. Learning to navigate these mixed feelings—without immediately trying to resolve them or deciding that one feeling must be "right" and the other "wrong"—is key to maintaining healthy, authentic connections.

The discomfort we often feel in the face of emotional complexity comes from our desire for clarity. We want our emotions to be straightforward, to tell a clear story. But the reality is that emotions are complex because life is complex. We experience loss and gain, love and pain, joy and sorrow, often in the same breath. By learning to sit with this complexity, we allow ourselves to experience life more fully. We don't have to rush to label our emotions or make sense of them immediately. Instead, we can simply acknowledge them as they are—messy, layered, and deeply human.

A powerful tool for navigating emotional complexity is self-reflection. When you notice that you are experiencing conflicting emotions, take a moment to sit with them. Write them down. Try to understand what each feeling is telling you. Often, different emotions reflect different needs or fears. For example, you might feel excitement about moving to a new city because you're eager for a fresh start, but also fear because you're leaving behind the comfort of what you know. Both emotions are valid, and both have important messages for you. By acknowledging each one, you can better understand what you need—perhaps a way to stay connected to old friends while embracing new opportunities.

Emotional complexity can also be a source of wisdom. It shows us that there is rarely a single right answer, that life is not black and white, but full of shades and layers. When we embrace our complex emotions, we develop greater empathy—not just for ourselves, but for others. We recognize that other people, too, are navigating their own blend of feelings, that they may be feeling joy and pain, hope and fear, all at once. This understanding helps us to be more compassionate, more patient, and more willing to see the humanity in others.

Ultimately, emotional complexity is a reminder that we are capable of holding many truths at once. We can be both strong and vulnerable, both confident and uncertain, both happy and sad. Our emotions do not have to fit neatly into categories, and they do not have to make sense to anyone but ourselves. By embracing the full spectrum of our emotions, by allowing them to coexist without judgment, we give ourselves permission to be fully human—to experience the richness, the depth, and the beauty of all that we feel.

Chapter 13: The Role of Emotions in Decision Making

Emotions play a critical role in decision-making, whether we are conscious of it or not. Despite our desire to view ourselves as rational beings, guided by logic and reason, the truth is that emotions significantly influence the choices we make every day. From the smallest decisions—like what to eat for breakfast—to the major, life-altering ones—like which career to pursue or whom to marry—emotions are always present. They serve as the undercurrent that guides our behavior, often in ways that are subtle but powerful.

Emotions help us prioritize. They inform us about what matters most to us, allowing us to weigh our options not just based on logical analysis but also on how each option makes us feel. When faced with multiple possibilities, emotions are the driving force that helps us decide which path resonates with our values, desires, and goals. This is why major life decisions are rarely made solely through cost-benefit analysis; they involve a sense of "rightness" that comes from an emotional connection to the choice.

Emotions also provide a kind of emotional compass, a gut feeling that often tells us what we need to know before our rational mind can fully process it. For instance, when we have a "bad feeling" about a person or situation, it is often our subconscious mind picking up on subtle cues that our conscious mind has not yet fully registered. This emotional feedback is invaluable because it gives us a more holistic view of the situation, incorporating information that isn't always clear-cut or easily quantifiable.

However, emotions can also lead us astray if we don't fully understand or acknowledge them. Acting out of fear can cause us to make overly cautious decisions, limiting our potential for growth and fulfillment. Anger, if left unchecked, can lead us to make impulsive decisions that we later regret. This is why emotional intelligence—our ability to recognize, understand, and manage our emotions—is so crucial in the decision-making process. Emotional intelligence allows us to differentiate between helpful emotions that can guide us toward a positive outcome and those that cloud our judgment.

Fear is one of the most common emotions that influences decision-making, and it can be both constructive and limiting. Fear can prevent us from making rash, dangerous choices, but it can also keep us from taking necessary risks. To make better decisions, we need to be able to distinguish between rational fears that serve a protective purpose and irrational fears that hold us back. By examining our fears, understanding where they come from, and challenging their validity, we can make more informed, balanced decisions.

Another important emotion in decision-making is desire. Desire drives us toward goals, gives us the motivation to pursue opportunities, and helps us to envision the kind of future we want for ourselves. But desire also needs to be balanced by practicality. Not all desires are worth pursuing, and not every dream can be realized in the way we imagine. The challenge is to honor our desires while also being realistic about the limitations we face. When making decisions, it is helpful to ask ourselves whether a particular course of action is aligned with our deepest values and whether the desire pushing us is one that will bring long-term fulfillment.

Love, too, is a significant emotional force in decision-making. It influences everything from the relationships we choose to maintain to the sacrifices we are willing to make for those we care about. Love can inspire us to act selflessly, to prioritize someone else's happiness above our own, and to make choices that we might not otherwise consider. But love, like all emotions, requires discernment. Loving someone does not mean losing yourself in the process, and decisions made purely out of love without consideration of your own needs can lead to resentment and imbalance.

The key to making decisions that honor both our emotions and our rational mind is to create space for reflection. When faced with a major decision, take the time to explore what you are feeling. What emotions are present? How are they influencing your thinking? Are they helping you see the situation more clearly, or are they clouding your judgment? By bringing these emotions into awareness, you can better understand their role in your decision-making process.

Mindfulness is a powerful tool in this regard. When we practice mindfulness, we learn to observe our emotions without immediately reacting to them. This creates a pause—a moment of reflection—that allows us to respond thoughtfully rather than impulsively. It is in this pause that we find the clarity needed to make decisions that align with both our values and our emotional needs.

Ultimately, emotions are not obstacles to decision-making; they are essential elements of it. They provide insight, motivation, and meaning. By embracing our emotions, understanding their influence, and learning to navigate them with awareness and intelligence, we can make decisions that are not only rational but also deeply fulfilling.

Chapter 14: Emotions and Relationships

Emotions are the lifeblood of our relationships. They shape how we connect with others, how we communicate, and how we navigate the inevitable challenges that arise in any human connection. Whether we are talking about friendships, romantic partnerships, family bonds, or professional relationships, emotions are always at play, influencing our actions and reactions, often in ways we might not even realize.

One of the most powerful emotions in relationships is empathy. Empathy allows us to understand and share the feelings of others, creating a bridge between our experiences and theirs. It is what enables us to be present for someone in their time of need, to celebrate their successes, and to truly connect on a deeper level. Empathy is not about fixing someone's problems or taking on their emotional burdens; it is about being with them, listening, and showing that we care. The presence of empathy in a relationship is often what makes the difference between feeling understood and feeling alone.

However, empathy can also be challenging. It requires emotional energy, and when we are overwhelmed by our own emotions, it can be difficult to be present for others. This is why self-care is an important aspect of maintaining healthy relationships. We cannot pour from an empty cup; to be there for others, we must first ensure that we are taking care of ourselves. Boundaries are also crucial in this regard. Setting boundaries does not mean that we care less; it means that we understand our limits and respect our own needs. Boundaries protect our well-being and, ultimately, enable us to show up more fully in our relationships.

Trust is another foundational emotion in relationships. Trust allows us to feel safe, to be vulnerable, to open ourselves to another person without fear of judgment or betrayal. It is built over time, through consistent actions, honesty, and reliability. When trust is broken, it is incredibly difficult to rebuild, but not impossible. It requires both parties to be willing to engage in honest dialogue, to take responsibility for their actions, and to work through the pain together. Trust is fragile, but when nurtured, it becomes the bedrock upon which strong, lasting relationships are built.

Love, in all its forms, is the emotion that binds relationships together. But love is not just a feeling; it is also a choice. It is the decision to show up for someone, to support them, to care for them even when it is difficult. Love requires effort. It requires us to communicate openly, to resolve conflicts with compassion, to forgive, and to grow together. In romantic relationships, love is often equated with passion, but true love goes beyond the initial spark. It involves a deep commitment, a willingness to work through challenges, and the ability to see and accept each other fully.

Conflict is inevitable in relationships, and the emotions that arise during conflict—anger, hurt, fear—can either drive us apart or bring us closer together, depending on how we handle them. Effective communication is key to navigating conflict in a healthy way. This means expressing our feelings honestly without blame, listening to understand rather than to defend, and being willing to find common ground. It also means managing our emotions so that they do not escalate the conflict but rather contribute to a constructive resolution. Anger, for example, can be a signal that something needs to change, but it must be expressed in a way that respects both ourselves and the other person.

Forgiveness is another essential aspect of emotional health in relationships. Holding onto anger, resentment, or bitterness can create a barrier that prevents true intimacy. Forgiveness does not mean forgetting or excusing harmful behavior; it means letting go of the desire for retribution and choosing to move forward. It is a gift we give not only to the other person but also to ourselves, freeing us from the emotional burden of holding onto pain.

Relationships also thrive on positive emotions—joy, gratitude, affection. These emotions reinforce the bond between people, creating a sense of shared happiness and fulfillment. Expressing gratitude, for example, is a powerful way to strengthen a relationship. When we take the time to acknowledge what we appreciate about someone, we not only make them feel valued, but we also remind ourselves of the reasons we care for them. Small acts of kindness, words of affirmation, and moments of shared laughter all contribute to the emotional richness of a relationship.

Ultimately, emotions are what make relationships meaningful. They allow us to connect on a deeper level, to share in each other's joys and sorrows, to grow together. By understanding and managing our own emotions, by practicing empathy, by communicating openly, and by nurturing the positive emotions that bring us closer, we can create relationships that are not only resilient but also profoundly fulfilling. Relationships are not always easy, but they are worth the effort, and it is through our emotional connections that we find true companionship and a sense of belonging.

Chapter 15: Emotional Healing and Growth

Emotional healing is not a linear process. It doesn't happen all at once, nor does it follow a straight path. It is an ongoing journey that requires patience, compassion, and a willingness to confront difficult feelings. Healing is about more than just "getting over" painful experiences; it's about integrating those experiences into the fabric of who we are, allowing them to become part of our story without defining us entirely. Emotional growth is about using these experiences as a foundation for transformation, becoming stronger, more resilient, and more compassionate as a result.

The first step in emotional healing is acknowledgment. We cannot heal from what we refuse to face. This means being honest about our pain—about what hurt us, about the impact it has had on our lives, about the ways in which we are still affected. It means allowing ourselves to feel whatever emotions arise—grief, anger, sadness, confusion—without judgment. Acknowledgment is about accepting that the pain is real, that it matters, and that it deserves our attention. It is only when we stop trying to suppress or ignore our feelings that true healing can begin.

Forgiveness is often a crucial aspect of emotional healing. Forgiveness is not about excusing harmful behavior or pretending that it didn't matter; it's about letting go of the anger, resentment, and bitterness that keep us tethered to the past. It's about freeing ourselves from the grip of pain so that we can move forward with our lives. Forgiveness may be directed towards others, but it is also about forgiving ourselves—letting go of the guilt, the "what ifs," and the self-blame that can hold us back. Forgiveness is an act of self-liberation, a decision to no longer allow past hurts to dictate our present and future.

Another important component of emotional healing is self-compassion. When we are hurting, it is easy to be harsh with ourselves—to blame ourselves for not being "strong enough" or for letting things affect us so deeply. But true healing requires us to treat ourselves with the same kindness and understanding that we would offer to a friend. Self-compassion is about recognizing that pain is part of the human experience, that there is no "right" or "wrong" way to heal, and that we are deserving of love and care, even in our most vulnerable moments.

Growth comes from our ability to learn from our experiences—to take the lessons of the past and use them to shape our future. Emotional growth is about becoming more self-aware, more understanding of others, and more resilient in the face of challenges. It's about recognizing patterns that no longer serve us—such as unhealthy coping mechanisms or self-destructive behaviors—and making a conscious effort to change them. Growth is not about perfection; it's about progress. It's about becoming a better version of ourselves, not despite our struggles, but because of them.

One of the most powerful tools for emotional growth is mindfulness. Mindfulness teaches us to be present with our emotions, to observe them without getting lost in them, and to respond rather than react. It helps us to break the cycle of automatic, often negative, responses to our emotions, allowing us to create space between stimulus and response. In this space, we find the freedom to choose a different path—a path that aligns with our values, our goals, and our true selves. Mindfulness also helps us to cultivate gratitude, even in the midst of difficulty. By focusing on what is good in our lives, we can begin to shift our perspective, finding light even in dark times.

Community and connection are also vital to emotional healing and growth. We are not meant to heal in isolation; we need others. Sharing our stories, our struggles, and our triumphs with others who understand creates a sense of belonging, reminding us that we are not alone. Whether it is through close friendships, support groups, therapy, or creative expression, connecting with others is a powerful way to facilitate healing. It is through these connections that we find validation, support, and encouragement—essential components of emotional resilience.

Healing and growth are lifelong processes. There will always be new challenges, new wounds, and new opportunities for growth. But by approaching these experiences with openness, by cultivating self-compassion, by learning from our past, and by seeking connection with others, we can continue to grow into the people we aspire to be.

Emotional healing is not about erasing pain but about transforming it—about turning wounds into wisdom, about finding strength in vulnerability, about becoming whole not in spite of what we have been through, but because of it.

Conclusion

Emotions are the threads that weave the fabric of our lives. They are the whispers of our deepest selves, the signals that guide us, the forces that shape who we are and how we connect with the world around us. To be fully human is to embrace the full spectrum of emotions—the joy, the fear, the love, the anger, the sorrow, the hope. It is to understand that emotions are not problems to be solved but experiences to be lived, understood, and integrated.

The journey through our emotional landscape is not always easy. It is messy, unpredictable, and at times deeply challenging. But it is also beautiful, enriching, and profoundly meaningful. By understanding our emotions, by allowing ourselves to feel them without judgment, by learning to navigate their complexity, we unlock the power to live authentically. We learn to connect with others on a deeper level, to make decisions that align with our values, and to grow in ways we never thought possible.

Embracing the full spectrum of emotions is not about always feeling good. It is about feeling fully. It is about allowing ourselves to experience life in all its richness—the highs, the lows, and everything in between. It is about seeing each emotion as a part of our journey, a part of who we are, and a part of what makes us human. By embracing our emotions, we embrace ourselves—our strengths, our vulnerabilities, our fears, our dreams. And in doing so, we find the courage to live a life that is true, meaningful, and deeply connected.

End Note

Life is an emotional journey—sometimes turbulent, sometimes serene, but always moving, always flowing. As you navigate your own journey, remember that every emotion you feel is valid. It is a part of your story, a part of your humanity. There is no need to fear the depths of your emotions or to strive for a life devoid of discomfort. Instead, strive for understanding, for compassion, for growth. Embrace the laughter, the tears, the rage, the quiet moments of contentment. Embrace it all. Because it is through feeling, through truly experiencing the spectrum of our emotions, that we find our way to a life that is not only lived but deeply, passionately, and authentically felt.